BAGGAGE BEYOND BIRKIN

Dating with Success After Divorce

A Modern Reference Guide & Interactive Workbook: Reclaim Your Confidence, Discernment, and Self-Worth

MARGOT GOLD

Disclaimer

The information provided in this book is for educational and informational purposes only. The author is not a licensed therapist, certified financial advisor, or legal professional.

While the strategies and insights shared are based on personal experience and research, they do not guarantee specific results in your dating life or financial situation. Relationship dynamics and financial recoveries are deeply personal and vary based on individual circumstances.

- Professional Advice: This book is not a substitute for professional counseling, therapy, or financial planning. If you are experiencing severe emotional distress or require complex legal or financial assistance regarding your divorce settlement, please consult a qualified professional.

- Liability: By reading this guide, you agree that the author and publisher are not responsible for any personal, emotional, or financial decisions made based on the content of this book.

- External Links: Any references to external resources, websites, or products are for convenience and do not imply endorsement.

- Birkin is a registered trademark of Hermès International S.A. This book is not affiliated with, or endorsed by, Hermès.

First Edition: 2026 Printed in Connecticut, USA

The Designer Glossary

***A Note from Margot:** Before you begin your journey, let's redefine the language of your life. In this reference guide and workbook, we don't use the words the world gave us; we use the ones we've earned.*

This glossary is just a fun, intentional way to look at our journey through a different lens. We aren't just "unpacking"; we're hand-picking a life that finally meets a higher standard—ours.

The Designer Original (Noun): She is a one-of-a-kind original who knows her worth isn't in spite of her past, but because of it. She doesn't audition for a role in someone else's life; she selects who earns a seat in hers.

The Designer Standard (Noun): The non-negotiable fabric of your life and relationships. This is the essential requirement for anyone seeking access to your space. If a connection doesn't fit the mold, it doesn't belong in your collection.

The Blueprint Check (Action): A deliberate look at the facts. It is the process of measuring a man's actual behavior against the standards you've set for your life. We don't ignore the flaws; we check the quality of the character before we invest our heart or our time.

The Baggage Reveal (Action): The moment you choose to put your cards on the table. It isn't a confession or an apology for your past; it's simply letting someone see the grit and wisdom that made you who you are today. It is the ultimate test of whether a partner has the emotional depth to appreciate a woman with a real history.

The Knock-Off (Noun): A person who looks the part at first but doesn't have the character to back it up. Like cheap imitation, they start to fall apart the moment things get real.

Mutual Selection (Mindset): The shift from "I hope he likes me" to "I am discerning if he is worthy of my time, peace, and history." You are an equal in the choosing process.

Table of Contents

Let's get started.

i. 💔 Introduction: A New Chapter Begins

This guide is for the woman who is ready to date again, on her terms. Without rushing. Without bitterness. And without compromising her peace.

You are not here to audition. You are here to discern.

A Note from Margot: *For a long time after my divorce, I carried my history like something I needed to apologize for. I worried that my life was "too much," too many years behind me, too much responsibility, too many pieces already lived. I felt like I had to minimize myself on dates.*

Then one night, sitting at my favorite local sushi spot, I met someone different. As I talked about my three kids, my work, and the chaos of managing a household, I braced for him to look overwhelmed.

Instead, he looked at me with genuine admiration and said, "That's incredible."

In that moment, something shifted. I realized that if I hadn't gone through my marriage and my divorce, I wouldn't have my children or the strength I built along the way. What I had been calling baggage was actually proof of what I could carry and create.

I stopped trying to prove myself and started asking a better question: Do I even like him?

If you haven't had that moment yet, we're going to find it together in these pages. Divorce does not diminish your value; it clarifies it. For years, many of us were "the glue" holding households and expectations together while our own needs faded into the background. Now, your time, your standards, and your clarity belong fully to you.

As you embark on this next chapter, remember: you are not "damaged goods." You are a **Designer Original.** Your history, your lessons, and your resilience are not a liability; they are your legacy. Let's flip the script together—this **"baggage" isn't a burden—it's your greatest asset**. It is how you detect red flags and build a safer, more intentional love.

The end of a marriage is a seismic shift, whether it was a choice you made or one that was made for you. But you didn't just "get through" it; you are here to decide what happens next.

How to Use This Guide

This is a reference guide and workbook designed to be revisited. Use the **First Date** and **Post-Date** tools

in real-time. Move through the prompts in the way
that serves you best.

What This Guide Will Help You Do
By the End of This Guide, You Will:

- **Own your story:** Get honest about the
  emotional and financial weight you're carrying.
  Learn to stop apologizing for your history and
  start recognizing it as the strength that protects
  your future.

- **Identify "Knock-Off" connections:** Use the 5-
  Point Blueprint Check to tell the difference
  between a man who is the real deal and
  someone who is just playing a part. Don't get
  distracted by a good first impression; make
  sure there's actual character behind it.

- **Establish a "Designer Standard":** Get clear on
  your deal-breakers before you even open the
  door to dating. This is about deciding exactly
  what it takes to be in your life. You are the one
  who decides who gets access to you; you don't
  wait to be chosen at a cost to yourself.

- **Flip the script on your past:** You aren't
  "damaged goods." Your history isn't something

to hide or apologize for, it's the actual evidence of what you're made of. It's the blueprint for the next chapter that finally meets your standard.

- **Own the "Mutual Selection" process:** Stop worrying about if they like you. Start focusing on whether they are worthy of your time and your peace. This isn't an audition; it's an evaluation. If they can't handle the depth of your history, they aren't the right fit.

- **Confidently execute a "Baggage Reveal":** Stop treating your history like a confession of what's wrong with you. Look at it as evidence of your strength. It's not about your flaws; it's about the hard-earned wisdom you've gained along the way.

Our time is the only thing you can't get more of, and this next phase is yours alone. But before you move forward, you must be honest: is your history going to be the weight that holds you back, or the very thing that allows you to set a higher standard? Turn the page to get real about what you're carrying. It's time to choose what's worth keeping and what you are finally ready to leave at the door.

ii. 🔓 Baggage Unpacked

After divorce, we all have baggage—and I'm not talking Birkin or Louis. We need to recognize that each of us carries a unique set of emotional and financial history stemming from our life experiences. Your baggage isn't something to hide or leave at the door; it's the proof of survival and lessons learned, and it's the blueprint that helps you spot the real thing when it shows up.

Your history is part of your value, but that doesn't mean you have to carry every single piece of it forever. Even the best of us need to look at our lives occasionally and decide what still fits. It's time to unpack, keep the lessons you've collected, and shed parts of yourself that no longer fit the vision for your future. You've lived the lessons; now, find a love that finally honors the depth of the woman you've become.

A Note from Margot: *There was a point during my divorce when I felt like a failure. It took time to realize that my marriage was good for the seasons it lasted, and when it wasn't, it was simply time to move into my next chapter. I don't look back with bitterness; I realize now that some things are built for a season, not a lifetime.*

Moving on wasn't always seamless. As a mom of three, dating an empty nester was a challenge. We were at a different stage in our lives, and there were times neither of us could compromise. Honestly? We shouldn't have had to. Learning to honor your own stage of life is a key part of maintaining your Designer Standard.

🧳 The History Behind the Standard

To build your "Designer Standard" future, we have to start by getting honest about the road you've already traveled.

- **The years that made you:** You've lived through decades of the good, the bad, and the exhausting. Every bit of that history—the joy, and the disappointment alike—is exactly what gave you the higher standards you have today.

- **The truth about divorce:** Divorce isn't a failure or a label you have to wear; it's just a chapter of your life. It's something you went through, not who you are.

- **The value in the cracks:** Stop looking at your "imperfections" as flaws. They are proof that you've lived and learned. Your history doesn't make you damaged; it's what makes you the genuine article.

💔 The Real Weight of Divorce:

Let's be honest: divorce is tough, especially when you're trying to shield your kids from the fallout. The emotional weight doesn't just disappear overnight; it stays with you for a while. If you need a professional to help you sort through the mess, take the help. It's not a sign of weakness; it's how you make sure you don't carry the unhealed wounds into your next chapter.

🤝 The Real Connection

The commitment: When you're honest about where you've been, you stop having to hide. That's how you build a relationship based on integrity: by showing him how the parts of your past make your present stronger. A high-quality relationship isn't about finding someone without a history; it's about choosing someone who respects you enough to help you build a future that matches your new standards.

Seeking Professional Help

- Whether it's therapy, counseling, or coaching, do the work if you need it. It's the only way to turn the hard stuff into wisdom that actually protects you.

- Seeking help is not a weakness; it's commitment to growth.

It takes two to build something real. While you're making peace with your own past, give yourself permission to look closely at his, too. You aren't being judgmental; you're just being careful with your heart.

Ask yourself: Does his baggage complement yours? If you decide it does, choose understanding, realizing that even the most high-value connections require grace and the willingness to meet halfway.

Introspection is vital; you must evaluate whether someone's emotional story aligns with your current capacity for support. Investing in yourself isn't a sign of lack; it is a commitment to your own personal growth and the ultimate sign of strength.

👵 Blueprint Profiles

Five women. Five stories of resilience.

Lois: The "Legacy" Unpacker

Age: *54 |* ***Stage:*** *Rediscovering her identity after 25 years of marriage.*

For over twenty years, Lois's life was defined by the roles she played: wife, mother, hostess, and the glue that held the family together. When she finally signed the papers, the silence in her house felt empty rather than peaceful as she had hoped. She felt like "damaged goods," worried that her best years had come and gone. To Lois, her "baggage" was the fear that she had waited too long to start over. She didn't realize yet that her years of resilience and her ability to build a beautiful life from scratch were the ultimate tools to design a future, one that she finally defined on her own terms.

Jackie: The "High-Powered" Unpacker

Age: *39 |* ***Stage:*** *Balancing a career, a social circle, and a new reality.*

From the outside, Jackie looked like she had it all: the career, the wardrobe, and the composure. But behind the scenes, her divorce felt like a crack in a façade she had spent a decade building. She spent her days juggling depositions and her nights wondering if people were whispering about her "failure" over brunch. Jackie used to think her perfectionism was the baggage that destroyed her marriage, and she hid her struggle to protect her image. Now, she's learning that her raw, honest self isn't a defect; it makes her a Designer Original. She's realized her honesty is her highest-value asset. She isn't looking for "perfect" anymore; she's selecting a partner whose baggage complements hers.

Maya: The "Pivot" Unpacker

Age: 31 | Stage: Navigating a "shorter" marriage and an unexpected reset.

Maya was young and thought she did everything right. She had the wedding, the starter home, and the five-year plan. When her marriage ended before their third anniversary, she felt like she was full of "what-ifs." To Maya, her baggage was the heavy sense of shame, the feeling that she had failed at the very start of her marriage and adult life. She looked at her friends' highlight reels and they looked so happy. Maya didn't realize yet that her "pivot" wasn't a setback; it was an early-access pass to a life to build on her own terms. Her asset wasn't just her youth; it was her courage to admit that her life looked good on paper but did not feel right in practice. Her hard-won wisdom was the foundation to finally start the life she wanted.

Amy: The "Betrayal" Unpacker

Age: *42 |* ***Stage:*** *Trust-Reset*

Amy's baggage isn't just divorce; it's the lingering hurt from betrayal. She lives on the "edge" in new relationships, always on the lookout for a shift in tone or a text that doesn't quite add up. She has moved past caring about status; what she needs now is emotional safety. She's not looking for showy gestures; she needs the quiet peace of consistency. Amy finally realized that being betrayed by her husband didn't make her "blind," it made her observant. She's learning how to trust again, without always expecting the worst.

Laurie: The "Accountable" Unpacker

Age: *48* | ***Stage:*** *New Foundation*

Laurie's baggage is the weight of her own choices. After her ten-year marriage ended following her own infidelity, she carried the heavy shame of hurting a good man and breaking up her family. After months of reflection, Laurie decided that her past would be a lesson, not a life sentence. She is human. She isn't just "moving on"; she is rebuilding herself from the lessons she has learned. By looking in the mirror and doing the hard work to heal her own heart, she is finally ready to build a life that is honest, solid, and built with integrity.

✅ The Blueprint Audit

Before we begin the work of unpacking, we must first identify what we are carrying. Use this space to align your journey with the women of the Blueprint Profiles.

The Alignment

Of the five Blueprint Profiles—Lois, Jackie, Maya, Amy, or Laurie - which woman's story feels like it was written for you?

Reflection:

____

____

____

____

(Is it her age, her professional pressure, the betrayal, hurt or her fear of the unknown that mirrors your own?)

The Connection

No matter which story speaks to you, the truth remains: your baggage isn't a burden to be hidden; it is the collection of experiences that prepared you for what's next.

Whether you feel the weight of a long-held history like Lois, the sting of interrupted plans like Maya, or the pressure to keep it all together like Jackie, you aren't unpacking alone. Amy and Laurie are moving through the same hard-won caution and quiet fresh starts. These women and their stories are here to walk through these pages with you, serving as a reminder that while the unpacking is personal, it doesn't have to be lonely. Use their breakthroughs as your blueprint and their tenacity as your guide.

Once you've cleared the emotional space, you need a solid place to stand. That starts with looking at the full picture of your assets.

iii. 💰 Beyond the Heart: Financial Heritage

Baggage extends beyond the emotional; it encompasses the financial. Divorce often forces an inventory of lost possessions and altered statuses, but your financial heritage is built on how you rebuild, not what was taken.

** When Lois looked at her bank balance after the settlement, it felt like she'd just signed away her best years. It took time for her to realize she wasn't waiting for someone else to approve the choices anymore; she was finally the one making them. As you look at your own history, ask yourself: Are you still looking back at the life you left, or are you finally claiming the one you're building?*

🏠 **The Heritage Assessment**

The Emotional Weight of Assets: Homes and possessions once tied to your security may now be memories. Acknowledge the loss but recognize that you are the one re-building; you have the Blueprints to build again.

- **Resilient rebuilding:** Income shifts and spousal support changes are simply temporary seasons. Rebuilding stability requires the same high-level determination you used to get through your divorce, a strength you already possess.

- **The Integrity test:** Financial hardship does not define your worth. A "Designer Standard" connection is built on compassion rather than judgment, creating emotional safety for both of you to grow.

The Transparency standard

- **Values over volume:** How you've handled money in the past is just part of your history. Being transparent about it isn't a weakness; it's the ultimate form of self-respect. It's the only way to make sure you aren't building a Designer Standard life on top of secrets that will eventually devalue everything you've worked for.

- **Shared currencies:** When merging lives, set joint goals and communicate expectations openly. Support each other's growth, as shared goals and teamwork create the most stable and deep connections.

The aftermath of divorce is an opportunity for rebuilding rather than dwelling on loss. Strength comes from navigating financial challenges and emerging stronger.

Transparency isn't just about numbers; it's about stability. When you're open about where you stand, you can plan a future together instead of just worrying about one. Don't ever confuse your bank balance with your worth. A temporary financial setback is just a repair in progress; it doesn't devalue the woman you are.

A Note from Margot: *I'll be honest, there were nights after my divorce when the house was finally quiet, and I sat at my kitchen table refreshing my bank app more than once, just to make sure the numbers hadn't somehow shifted. I wasn't buying anything extravagant. I was calculating groceries, school expenses, basics. When I signed a lease in only my name for the first time, my hand actually paused before I put pen to paper. It wasn't just about the* *money. It was the realization that I was the only one holding the pen now.*

That was the moment I realized no one else was coming to handle it for me. It was uncomfortable and honestly, a little scary. But it was also clarifying.

If you're in that season of checking your account before you swipe your card, I want you to hear this: a number on a screen does not measure your worth. The fact that you're showing up and figuring it out anyway—that's the real strength.

Your financial history is a piece of the puzzle, and you're still putting the rest of the picture together. But even while your new chapter is still taking shape, you deserve to live by your standards right now. You don't have to wait until you're perfectly settled to start setting higher standards. Next is the Quality Control Check, the tools you need to vet new connections while you continue to build the life you deserve. Now that your own foundation is clear, let's look at how to spot that same integrity in others.

iv. 🔷 Redefining Love: The Quality Control Check

Society sells us the "glossy" version of love—one that looks impressive from a distance but doesn't have the substance to handle the real world. Real love isn't a checklist of height, age, or tax brackets. It's a connection that holds up because it's built on the things that don't go out of style: your shared values.

Auditing for durability

🚫 Ditch the Prototype: Stop shopping for a "type." Many high-value connections don't begin with instant sparks; they begin with mutual respect and emotional intelligence. Challenge your assumptions about your "type" around height, age, or appearance, and let go of standards that don't actually predict long-term fulfillment.

A Note from Margot: I'm barely 5'3 in the morning; do I really need to be with a 6'4 man? Probably not. What is one "must-have" physical trait you've been shopping for that actually has nothing to do with the quality of a man's heart?

- 🌈 **Heritage over hype:** If you are in a mature chapter of life, a successful match isn't found in someone decades younger who can't speak your language. It's found in a partner who shares your pace, your depth of experience, and your uncompromising vision for your future.

- ✅ **High-quality character:** You're looking for a man who doesn't fall apart the second life gets complicated. We aren't interested in the guys who are only great when things are easy and the "newness" is high. You want the kind of character that stays solid even when the honeymoon phase ends.

- 🤍 **Vulnerability:** The Mark of Substance True vulnerability is impossible to fake, especially in an era of surface-level swiping. It isn't a weakness; it's the evidence of your depth. While many lean on a polished persona, your willingness to be seen is the very thing that proves your value.

🧳 The Baggage Reveal:

- Sharing your truth is how you invite a high-quality partner to do the same.
- It's not about dumping trauma; it's about showing the "collection of life experiences" that made you who you are today.

💡 The Reality premium:

Authentic connection requires staying in the real world. It's a shift from chasing teenage fantasies to finding a love that is steady and deliberate. We aren't looking for a movie moment—we are selecting a partnership that holds up when life gets complicated.

A Note from Margot: I once went on at least five dates with a man I felt no immediate physical attraction to, but I was drawn to his intelligence and kindness. By the seventh date, something shifted. The spark wasn't forced; it grew. What I later recognized was that feeling seen, valued, and genuinely admired created a kind of attraction I had underestimated.

V. 🌷 Conclusion: Loving After Divorce

Everyone carries *baggage,* and in this new chapter, we acknowledge it as a mark of a life lived. The key to dating after divorce isn't avoiding your history; it's choosing a partner whose **baggage** complements your own.

The Heritage Connection is when two people accept each other's past and create a partnership that is:

- **Grounded in truth:** A relationship built on genuine honesty rather than the shimmer of a first impression. It's about choosing a connection that is real and transparent over one that just looks good on the surface.

- **Resiliently aligned:** A connection that protects the peace and the value of the baggage of the women we've become.

- **Rooted in understanding:** A love that doesn't ask you to "unpack and hide," but rather finds a perfect fit for the life you've built. When two people accept each other's past, they create a love that is enduring, real, and rooted in understanding.

The Integrity Filter: Dating after divorce isn't about finding perfection; it's about identifying a connection that is as unwavering as you are. If your history feels "too heavy" for someone to manage, they simply aren't equipped to stand beside you in the life you are building.

Keep your standards high, your heart open, and your history honored. You aren't just dating; you are intentionally selecting the partner who deserves a place in your future.

You now have the vision. You have the heart. Now, it is time to set your new standard. The following pages are your Designer's Workbook, a private space to draft, shape, and own your future. You've reflected on your past and reframed your story; now, it's time to apply that clarity in real time.

vi. 📋 The 5-Point Blueprint Check

The 5-Point Blueprint is more than a guide for dating; it is the solid framework for your next chapter. After a major life shift like divorce, it is tempting to rush into a "makeover," focusing on the surface to hide the messy parts. But a woman who values her peace knows that even the most beautiful life will eventually feel unstable if it is built on a weak foundation.

This Blueprint is designed to help you look at your life and decide exactly what, and who, is worthy of a place in your future. We are moving away from seeking approval and toward a position of intentional selection.

You aren't just looking for a connection; you are vetting a partner for the most significant role in your life. Use these five pillars to ensure your next build is as solid as it is intentional.

1. **Integrity:** Did his actions match his profile (The Digital Showroom vs. Reality)?

2. **Material quality:** Did the conversation have depth, or was it "Knock-Off" small talk?

3. **The pace check:** Is he rushing the connection, or respecting the Designer Standard timeline?

4. **Baggage response:** If a "Baggage Reveal" happened, did he handle it with high-end maturity or "budget" judgment?

5. **Mutual selection:** Do I actually *like* him, or am I just relieved he likes me?

The 5-Point Blueprint Check (Post-Date Evaluation)

Date Name: ______________________   Date Number:
[1] [2] [3]

1.   **Visual vs. reality:** Did he match his "Digital Showroom" (profile), or was he a bait-and-switch? [Yes / No]

2.   **Integrity:** Did he ask about my life/goals, or was the conversation 100% about his "features"? [Yes / No]

3.   **The peace test:** Do I feel energized and "light," or am I mentally "re-packing" my baggage to fit his needs? [Yes / No]

4.   **Boundary response:** I set a small boundary tonight (time, location, or topic). How did he react?

        (A) Respectfully (B) Dismissively (C) Aggressively

5.   **The designer verdict:** Is he a "Designer Standard" investment, or a "dupe" that will fall apart by next month? [Yes / No]

vii. ⬇️ The Digital Showroom (Dating Apps)

Think of dating apps as a high-volume showroom. You wouldn't buy a car without a test drive, and you shouldn't dismiss a potential partner without a "vibe check."

A Note from Margot: *At the start of my post-divorce journey, I was terrified of being seen. I'd open a dating app and feel a wave of embarrassment that someone I knew might spot me and close it immediately. My heart was racing. I felt like I was standing on a shelf, waiting to be judged. But I eventually realized there is no reason to be embarrassed for choosing to live again.*

- **The pro-app logic:** Why limit your reach? Apps give you access to a global landscape of potential partners you'd never cross paths with at your local coffee shop or gym. It's not "desperate"; it's **strategic.**

  **I know how intimidating it feels to put yourself "on a shelf" in an app after years of marriage. I've been there, and that first swipe really is the hardest. I remember an awkward Cup of Joe meetup when I found out the man I was* *meeting had grabbed coffee with one of my friends the day before. In the moment, it stung—but later I realized it wasn't a big deal at all. Dating apps work for me because I'm not a bar person, life gets busy, and going out gets expensive.*

- **The "Quick Cup of Joe" rule:** A suggestion to hold off on the three-course dinner with a stranger on your first date. Meet in a bright, public space for a 30-minute coffee. It's a low-investment way to see if the "authentic connection" is there before you commit your most valuable asset: **your time.**

  ** I started using the 30-minute coffee rule because, as a busy mom, my time with my kids is my "most precious asset" I won't waste on a three-course dinner with a mismatched connection.*

- **The chemistry myth:** In a world of instant swipes, we've forgotten that real chemistry can be gradual, not a lightning strike. If he's a great guy with solid values, give him a second date.

High-quality resilience often looks like "steady and safe" rather than "flashy and fast."

Some of my strongest relationships were with men I had no physical attraction to at first, and I'm glad I gave it a chance. Chemistry is not always immediate.

- **The "in-person" mindset:** Treat a digital match with the same grace you'd give someone you met through a friend. We give more chances to people in person because we see their humanity. Force yourself to look for humanity behind the screen.

  Even if I didn't see a match, I always had the grace to enjoy good company and to be kind, meeting good people is a positive.

- **A space for intentionality:** Apps give you the opportunity to lead with your Designer Standard. Because you can see a person's "profile" before speaking, seek out those who acknowledge their past and life lessons. As seen in Maya's Pivot, apps can be an "early-access pass" to a life built entirely on your own terms.

It's a personal choice but I never swiped for anyone who didn't write a profile. If he didn't have time to share why his baggage may complement mine, then how can he be my Designer Standard Match?

- **Control over the pace:** Users can decide how quickly or slowly they want to move, from the initial "swipe" to the first "Quick Cup of Joe." This puts the user in the driver's seat of their own new chapter.

I was able to jump on an app anytime, anywhere, in dirty sweats, and as often or as rarely as I want. It is convenient.

- **Safety**: Features like in-app messaging and video calls allow for a "vibe check" before sharing personal contact information or meeting in person. This helps ensure a level of comfort and safety before committing time to a date.

My children's safety and my own security are non-negotiable; this approach allowed me to vet connections without compromising either.

- **Access to like-minded individuals**: Niche apps or specific filters can help people find partners who share unique interests, religious views, or lifestyle choices (like fitness or "foodie" culture) that might be hard to identify in a random encounter.

  This saves a lot of time with unnecessary Quick Cup of Joe.

- **A greenhouse for growth:** Apps are a "vibe check" for your own soul. They provide a space to practice being real and test your personal non-negotiables in a high-volume environment. As Maya realized, the app isn't a sign of lagging behind; it's an "early-access pass" to a life built on your own terms.

  After my divorce, I wanted to get out of my bubble. Using the apps allowed me to cast a wide net and get a real feel for the dating landscape without wasting time.

Time for a blueprint check—is his profile an original or a Knock-Off?

viii. 💎 The Authenticity Test: Real vs. Knock-Off

Step 1: The Quality Control Checklist

A Blueprint tells you if a connection is safe to enter; an Authenticity Test tells you if it's a place you want to be. We start with the Blueprint to protect your time, and we follow with The Authenticity Test to protect your heart.

By this stage, he has passed your initial filters. He's shown up, he's consistent, and he has met the basic requirements you set in your "Digital Showroom."

But as anyone who has moved through the dating world knows, an imitation can look perfect from a distance. He may have the right look and say all the right things, but the true value isn't in the outward appearance, it's in how his character holds up over time and under pressure.

Now that you've confirmed he is reliable and solid, it's time to look at the substance. This isn't about his resume or his "specs"; it's about his integrity. We are looking for the "genuine" qualities that define a partner of true depth. Before you invest your heart, look closely at who he really is.

Use these benchmarks to distinguish between a man of real character and one who is simply playing the part. This is how you ensure he truly meets your Designer Standard.

The Backstory check (transparency vs. secrecy)

- **The Authentic Hallmark:** He speaks about his past with "Emotional Clarity." He takes ownership of his history and explains his growth without bitterness.

- **The Knock-Off trait:** He uses status (cars, job titles) to hide a lack of emotional depth or to deflect from his "broken hardware."

The Consistency test (durability vs. flash)

- **The Authentic Hallmark:** His actions match his words. This is the enduring quality of a man whose character only becomes more impressive the longer you know him.

- **The Knock-Off trait:** He is "flashy and fast," creating a cinematic fantasy he can't sustain once the "newness" wears off.

The Vulnerability audit (real vs. surface-level version of love)

- **The Authentic Hallmark:** He isn't afraid to show his "scuffs", the hard moments that add character to his life.

- **The Knock-Off trait:** He sells a "no-baggage claim" that feels surgically sterile and emotionally hollow.

Like Amy, you aren't looking for reasons to leave; you're simply checking the weight of a man's word before you let him into your life. This isn't cynicism; it's the quiet work of protecting your peace.

Step 2: Now, apply what you've learned. Think of the person you are currently dating and check the box that best describes their "structural integrity."

Feature	Knock-Off Trait (🚩 Red Flag)	Authentic Connection (✅ Green Flag)
Baggage Talk	Blames the ex, unresolved weight.	Acknowledges their part; lessons considered.
Past/Status	Uses money/status to avoid depth.	Open about reality and emotional goals.
Consistency	High intensity early; fades fast.	Steady follow-through, slow burn
Self-Image	Projecting a "perfect," sterile life.	Embraces imperfections and character.
Presence	Transactional; "What can you do for me?"	Values your peace; seeks to add value.

The result: * Mostly Green: A "Designer Standard" partnership worthy of your presence.

Any red: Proceed with caution. Remember, your time is invaluable; don't spend it on a "Knock-Off"!

Jackie initially struggled with a "Knock-Off" life because of her perfectionism. Use her as a reminder that being "authentic" means embracing the character of a life well-lived, not a "no-baggage" claim.

ix. 🐝 First Date Guide: Curating Connection

A first date isn't an interview; it's a "vibe check." Your goal is to see if their baggage is organized and if it is ready for the quality of connection you offer. Use these prompts to move past small talk without diving too deep into the "heavy stuff" too soon.

Some women often feel like they need to be "picked" when they re-enter the dating world. We need to shift that mindset to one of Mutual Selection: I pick you, and you pick me. Go into every date knowing exactly who you are and the value you bring to the table. Look at what you've been through; you've navigated a divorce and reclaimed your power. You are a Designer Original never settle for a "Knock-Off" connection.

✦ Phase 1: The Light reveal (establishing transparency)

Instead of asking "Why did you get divorced?", try these to see how they view their past:

- What's one thing you've learned about yourself since becoming single that surprised you? *(Checks for: Self-awareness).*

- What does your "peace" look like these days? *(Checks for: If they have done the emotional work to find stability).*

- What's a passion you've rediscovered lately that you'd put on the shelf for a while? *(Checks for: Independence and zest for life).*

- What's a "small win" you've had this week that made you feel like you're exactly where you're supposed to be? *(Checks for: Positivity and the ability to find joy in the present moment.)*

- If you had a completely free Saturday with no obligations, what would a planned day look like? *(Checks for: Compatibility of pace and personal interests.)*

- What is one "non-negotiable" for your peace that you've established in this chapter of your life? *(Checks for: Boundaries and emotional maturity.)*

** Yours might be If a man texts you for the first time at 11:00 PM, you don't owe him a response. By choosing your own rest over a low-effort connection, you aren't being difficult; you are simply upholding **the Designer Standard.***

💼 Phase 2: The "Baggage" soft check (assessing compatibility)

You don't need their tax returns or a therapy transcript on day one. Look for how they manage life's complexities:

- I've realized that life after divorce is a lot about rebuilding. What's been the most rewarding part of your "new chapter" so far? *(Checks for: Growth mindset vs. a victim mindset).*

- I value transparency. How do you usually handle it when things get a little complicated in life? *(Checks for: Communication styles).*

- I like to think of my life post-divorce as having my bags finally packed and organized. How would you describe the space you're in right now? Are you living in a place that feels open and ready for someone new, or is there still a lot of "moving day" chaos going on with your past? *(Checks for: Is he emotionally available, or is his headspace still crowded by his ex?)*

- We've both lived some life. What's one piece of the past you're proud to have finally unpacked and left behind? *(Checks for: Self-reflection and the ability to release the past.)*

- When you think about an Ideal Partnership, what is the one quality you value most that you didn't prioritize in your 20s? *(Checks for: Evolution of standards and maturity.)*

- How do you balance maintaining your own time with friends/hobbies while building a new connection? *(Checks for: Independence and healthy relationship boundaries.)*

🔍 The Clarity Filter

- **The blame game:** If they spend more than 10 minutes talking about how "crazy" an ex was, their baggage is unorganized and leaking into your space.

- **The "No baggage" claim:** Beware the man who insists everything is perfect; a lack of self-reflection is the ultimate Knock-Off trait.

- **The "And" factor:** Celebrate a partner who can acknowledge that divorce was hard *and* they are happy now, this is the hallmark of a high-quality, resilient heritage.

- **Respectful boundaries:** A true "Designer Standard" partner shares enough to be real but doesn't dump their "trauma baggage" before the appetizers arrive.

** Your time is luxury. If a date isn't a match, it isn't a failure, it's just a step closer to the person whose baggage fits perfectly in your overhead compartment.*

X. The Founder's Fuel: Moving for Your Peace

You've moved past the digital showroom, decoded the "Knock-Off" profiles, and sat through the 30-minute coffee vibe-checks. Whether those dates were successful or felt like a total waste of your best outfit, one thing is certain: building a life that fits you is high-energy work, and you may need to refuel.

Your body is the vessel for your comeback. While I personally find my strength on the elliptical and my peace in a post-workout meal, your "movement" doesn't have to look like mine to be effective.

The goal isn't a "revenge body"; it's a resilient mind. When you've been carrying the weight of a divorce, physical movement serves as a literal way to "unpack" the stress that settles on your shoulders and your heart.

A Note from Margot: Some days my workouts were half-finished, but showing up anyway gave my mind somewhere to land when everything else felt unsettled.

The Resilient Movement Philosophy:

- **Movement is an "emotional reset" for your soul:** Use exercise to clear the mental clutter before a date or a tough conversation. It centers you on your own worth before you step into someone else's space.

- **Reclaim your time:** Use your workout as a boundary. It is a dedicated appointment with yourself where you are the priority.

- **The slow burn approach:** Just like real love, physical progress is a slow burn. Whether it's a 20-minute walk or a yoga flow, consistency is what builds the mental stamina you need for this next chapter.

- **Reward your hard efforts:** I believe in the power of a workout followed by an even better meal. Treat yourself to a favorite dish as a celebration of what your body can do.

Your inventory:

What is one form of movement you've "put on the shelf" that you're ready to rediscover?

How can you use movement this week to respect your own "peace"?

xi. The Unpacking Session: Reflection Prompts

A woman of substance knows that before she can manage how the world sees her, she must maintain a clear and honest understanding of her own history. You cannot strategically share your story with a partner until you have first made peace with it yourself. You cannot decide which parts of your past are worth keeping and which need to be left behind until you are willing to look at them with total honesty.

Unpacking is not about rummaging through the mistakes of your past; it is a high-level evaluation. Every experience you've had, every misaligned relationship, every setback, and every season where you felt undervalued, has contributed to the person you are today.

In this section we are going to examine these experiences one by one. We aren't looking for blame; we are looking for the lessons hidden beneath the surface. Use these prompts to discern which parts of your history are weights that hold you back, and which are the hard-won insights that make you who you are.

Take a breath. Open the space. Let's see what we're working with.

1.   The Private Inventory: What are the three heaviest items in your emotional baggage right now?

____

____

____

(e.g., If you're unsure, look back at Maya. Her heaviest item was the shame of a "failed" five-year plan. Is your weight similar, or are you carrying a 'Legacy' weight like Lois?)

2.   Look at the item you listed above, what strength has it forced you to develop?

____

____

____

(e.g., If your baggage is "financial fear," your asset is "becoming a master of your own wealth.")

3.   The Maintenance: What is one specific way you have "upgraded" your baggage since your divorce?

____

____

____

4.   The Financial narrative: How can you reframe your financial baggage into a story of resilience and heritage?

____

____

____

5.   The Future set: What does a typical Tuesday afternoon feel like in a healthy, shared-baggage relationship?

____

____

____

6.   Is his "baggage" organized enough to fit into the life I've built, or would it create clutter I no longer want?

____

____

____

7.   I'm a big believer in rewarding tenacity. What's your favorite way to celebrate a personal breakthrough? (Checks for: Shared values around self-care and celebration.)

____

____

____

8.   What's a goal you're currently "blueprinting" for your future that has nothing to do with work or family? (Checks for: Personal ambition and a sense of purpose outside of roles like "mother" or "employee".)

____

____

____

The Retirement Ceremony

Official retiring of the compromised mindset

A Designer Original knows when a certain element no longer has a place in her life. Some memories are meant to be kept as wisdom, while others are simply outdated patterns taking up space in your creative field.

Below, name one piece of "baggage" a belief, a label an ex gave you, or a fear that you are officially retiring today. You are not "throwing it away" in a panic; you are gracefully decommissioning it because it is no longer up to your Standard.

I, [   ], the Founder and CEO of my own life, hereby retire:

____

____

____

Reason for retirement: (e.g., *Outdated, unsound, or no longer fits the Designer Standard.*)

The Replacement: (What new "Designer Original" belief is taking its place?)

Signed: _________________ Date: _________________

Now that you've turned your baggage into your legacy, you're standing on solid ground. You aren't apologizing for your history anymore; you're owning it. But owning it doesn't mean giving it away for free. Let's talk about how to use this new strength as a filter to see who is actually worthy of your time.

xii. 🧳 The Baggage Reveal Strategy

***This worksheet helps you move from "confessing"
to "communicating" your value.***

The Baggage Reveal isn't a confession; it's a quality check. You've already done the internal work to reframe your story; now it's time to apply the 'Wait-and-See' Gauge to the man sitting across from you. This is where we see if his character matches your standard.

A Note from Margot: *Earlier in my dating, someone told me I was "a mystery." At first, I took it as a compliment. But the truth was, I wasn't mysterious; I was guarded. After my divorce, I didn't know how to share my story without feeling exposed or judged, so I kept things polished and surface-level. I thought protecting myself meant staying quiet about the heavy parts.*

It wasn't until I slowly shared pieces of my history with someone who had earned my trust that I felt the difference. I didn't feel weak. I felt seen. And I realized vulnerability isn't about telling everything—it's about sharing honestly with someone who has shown they can handle it.

I hope this Baggage Reveal strategy helps you do the same, not for fear of losing someone, but from confidence in your worth.

There is a specific kind of weight we carry when we feel responsible for the ending of our last chapter. It's easy to feel like you've been disqualified from the Designer Standard because your hands aren't perfectly clean.

**But remember Laurie? She spent years carrying the shame of her choices, feeling like her past was a permanent stain on her character. It wasn't until she started her "New Foundation" phase that she realized her history was a lesson, not a life sentence. Like Laurie, your value isn't found in a "perfect" track record; it's found in the radical honesty and integrity you've built since then. Owning your mess doesn't make you less desirable—it makes you a woman who knows the true value of the truth.*

You have checked his Blueprint. You have refueled your own vessel. Now, it's time to see if you're standing on the same ground. We all have history. But as a One-of-a-Kind Original, your history isn't something to hide, it's the very thing that adds to your value. But not everyone is qualified to hear it. Before we begin Unpacking the past to him, we must master

the Baggage Reveal: the art of knowing when to stay
closed, when to share, and how to tell your story as
an asset, not an apology.

Look back at your Unpacking Session. Pick the three pieces you are most likely to encounter in a real conversation (like the kids or the ex). Then, let's polish them for the reveal.

Part 1: Presentation pieces

List three "heavy" pieces of your history (e.g., your divorce details, co-parenting challenges, or career pivots).

1. ____

2. ____

3. ____

Part 2: The Reframing

Next to each item, write the Designer Asset it created.

> *e.g., "Messy Divorce" becomes "Expert-level Conflict Resolution and Boundaries."*

1. ____

2. ____

3. ____

Part 3: The "Wait-and-See" gauge

Before you reveal, answer these three "Designer Standard" questions:

- **Consistency:** Has he shown up on time and stayed true to his word for at least three dates? [Yes / No]

- **Emotional safety:** Does he listen more than he speaks, or does he interrupt? [Listen / Interrupt]

- **The "Knock-Off" test:** Does he judge others' "baggage" when he talks about his past? [Yes / No]

The Rule: If you answered "No" to any of these, pause the reveal. He hasn't yet earned the right to your history.

xiii. 👜 The Designer Standard: Post-Date Quality Control

The Final inspection

The Mindset check: Before you begin this assessment, ensure you are not looking through the lens of your past patterns. You're putting your life back together, intentionally.

The Final vetting: You have checked the Blueprint for safety. You have refueled your own tank. You have even sorted through your own history in the Unpacking Session. Now, it's time for the final moment of selection.

Sometimes something looks good at first. But before you let it into your life, take a breath and look closer. Does it still feel right when you slow down?

We are checking the compatibility of your lives, the consistency of his character, and, most importantly, how your energy feels when it is paired with his.

The Rule of selectivity: If the alignment is off by an inch today, the relationship will be off by a mile in a year. Be intentional. Your life only has room for quality that matches your own.

The Designer Standard: Post-Date Quality Control Checklist

Date Name/Date: ______________________

Drive Home: *On the drive home, don't just check your list. Check your peace. Did your heart feel lighter or heavier after that coffee?*

The "Open book" policy

- **Consistency Check:** Did his actions match his words? (e.g., He showed up on time and followed through on plans).

- **The Past Talk:** Did he acknowledge his part in his divorce rather than blaming an ex for everything?

- **Authenticity Score:** ☐ Authentic (Self-aware) | ☐ Knock-Off (Blame game).

The "Heavy lifting" test

- **Initiative Check:** Did he take the lead in "building" the connection, or did you do the emotional labor?

- **Value-Add:** Did he show active listening by asking about your rediscovered passions or your "new chapter"?

- **Authenticity Score:** ☐ Authentic (Value-add) | ☐ Knock-Off (Empty suit/Surface-level).

The "No-filter" respect

- **Vibe Check:** How did he handle the world around him (service staff, stress, or minor glitches)?

- **Boundaries: Did** he share enough to be real without "dumping" unresolved trauma before the appetizers?

- **Authenticity Score:** ☐ Authentic (Grounded) | ☐ Knock-Off (Lacks honesty/reflection).

Remember Jackie's tendency toward the "Knock-Off" life? Did your date tonight feel like a Designer Standard connection, or were you masking your reality like Jackie once did?

The Final Check: (check off)

[ ] **The real deal:** He has substance. It's time to move toward the **Baggage Reveal**.

[ ] **The mixed bag:** He has potential, but the red flags (or yellow ones) are visible. Proceed with a **"Trial Period"** only, keep your eyes open.

[ ] **The mistake:** This isn't what you're looking for. Time for an **immediate return** to your own life and priorities.

xiv. 📝 A Note to Men

If you've picked up this guide, chances are you aren't just looking for a date; you're looking for a partnership that has some substance behind it.

After a divorce, it's easy to think that your past is a liability. But in the world of Baggage Beyond Birkin, we see it differently. Your history, your baggage, is what gives you the depth, and the character that a high-value woman is looking for.

To meet her at the Designer Standard, remember:

- **Organize your inventory:** Take ownership of your past. A man who can acknowledge his role in his previous chapter without bitterness is the ultimate real connection.

- **Protect the peace:** Understand that the woman you are dating has spent years curating her own life and peace. Don't just enter her space; respect it.

- **Value over flash:** You don't need a perfect story or a "no-baggage" claim. You just need the integrity to be real and the transparency to be trusted.

When you've organized your baggage and you know exactly what you're looking for, you stop being just another "option"—you become the standard.

xv. About the Author

About Margot Gold

Margot Gold is a Designer Original too, a mother of three, and a woman who knows exactly what it feels like to sit at the kitchen table wondering how to rebuild a life from the ground up. She understands the "beautiful chaos" of balancing a career and a family.

Margot learned that a Designer Standard life isn't about being perfect, it's about being intentional. She discovered that the most fulfilling chapters aren't found by accident; they are built, piece by piece, with patience and a clear sense of purpose.

Driven by a genuine heart for connection, Margot has always been the one to create the community she wished she had. Whether she was leading a local book club or a running group, she knew that no one needed to navigate a new chapter alone; they should have a choice. She authored this book to be the companion she once searched for, a bridge to a sisterhood of women reclaiming their worth together.

When she isn't cheering on her kids or supporting her community, Margot is a true believer in the power of a long workout followed by an even better meal. She loves her tuna sashimi, fresh oysters, and a perfectly cooked steak. Her mission is simple: to help you recognize your inherent value, embrace your history, and find a love that is as genuine and formidable as you are.

A Note from Margot: *The Standard Has Been Set*

If you are reading this, you have already done the hardest part: you have stopped looking at your history as a deficit and started seeing it as your signature advantage.

Dating after divorce isn't about "getting back out there." It is about honoring the life you are rebuilding, it is now so well-aligned that only the most genuine, high-integrity connections are invited into your inner circle.

Remember, your lived lessons have made you singular and rare. Your history is the quiet knowing that ensures you make the best decisions for your future. Never compromise on what you deserve and never settle for a "Knock-Off" connection again.

You're not looking for someone to finish your life anymore. You've already built it. Now you're deciding who gets to be part of it.

Welcome to your next chapter.

The Baggage Beyond Birkin Community

As you unpack, keep what serves you and release what no longer fits. You've moved through the complexities of divorce and come out on the other side. You will thrive in this new chapter. Will you make mistakes? Of course. But you will add those lessons to your baggage.

Remember, your history is your most powerful blueprint. If the depth of your experience feels "too heavy" for someone else, they simply lack the capacity to meet the Designer Standard.

You don't have to unpack alone. Stay connected to a camaraderie of women who share a common thread of redefining their worth. We go beyond the scenes to discuss the real strategies for a post-divorce life. Join us for daily inspiration, support, and the kind of connection that is as rare as it is enduring.

Join the Baggage Beyond Birkin Community:

Facebook:
https://www.facebook.com/groups/baggagebeyondbirkinbaggageunpacked

https://www.facebook.com/baggagebeyondbirkin

Instagram:
https://www.instagram.com/baggagebeyondbirkin/

Connect with Margot

Ready to take the next step in your own evolution? Margot is available for coaching and speaking engagements to help you navigate your post-divorce chapter with clarity and strength.

For coaching inquiries or speaking engagements, please reach out to Margot at: baggagebeyondbirkin@gmail.com

www.ingramcontent.com/pod-product-compliance
Lightning Source LLC
Chambersburg PA
CBHW040827120726
48005CB00012B/1526